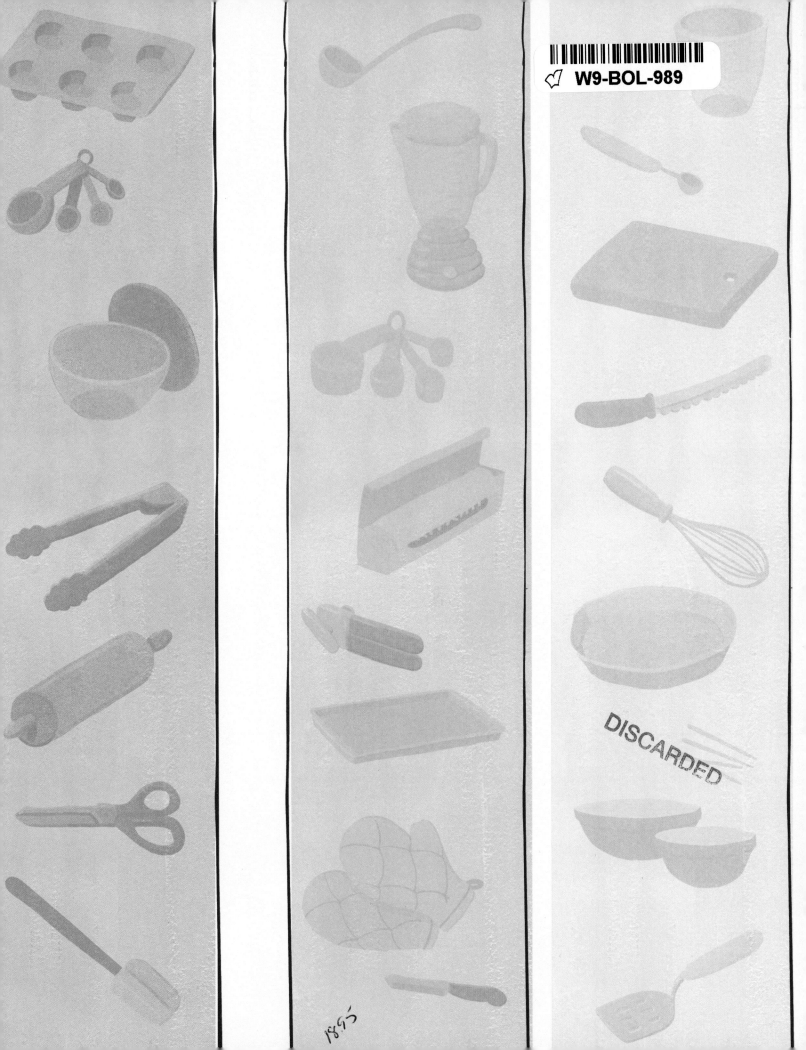

W9-BOL-989

DISCARDED

1895

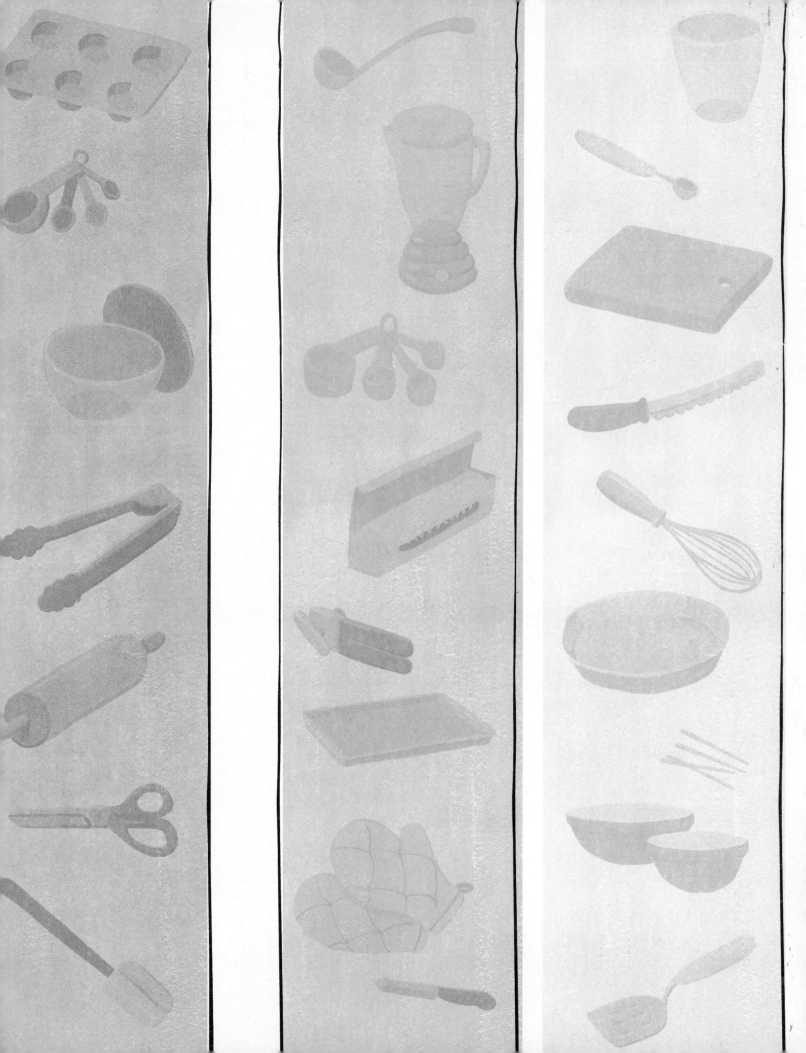

Keep on Rollin' Meatballs

and Other Delicious Dinners

by Nick Fauchald   illustrated by Rick Peterson

Special thanks to our content adviser:
Joanne L. Slavin, Ph.D., R.D.
Professor of Food Science and Nutrition
University of Minnesota

PICTURE WINDOW BOOKS
Minneapolis, Minnesota

Editors: Christianne Jones and Carol Jones
Designer: Tracy Davies
Page Production: Michelle Biedscheid

Art Director: Nathan Gassman
The illustrations in this book were created with acrylics and gouache.

The illustration on page 5 is from *www.mypyramid.gov*.

Copyright © 2008 by Picture Window Books
All rights reserved. No part of this book may be reproduced without written permission from the publisher. The publisher takes no responsibility for the use of any of the materials or methods described in this book, nor for the products thereof.

Printed in the United States of America

 All books published by Picture Window Books are manufactured with paper containing at least 10 percent post-consumer waste.

Library of Congress Cataloging-in-Publication Data
Fauchald, Nick.
Keep on rollin' meatballs : and other delicious dinners / by Nick Fauchald ; illustrated by Rick Peterson.
p. cm. — (Kids dish)
Includes index.
ISBN 978-1-4048-3998-4 (library binding)
1. Dinners and dining—Juvenile literature. I. Peterson, Rick. II. Title.
TX737.F387 2008
641.5—dc22   2007032926

Editors' note: The author based the difficulty levels of the recipes on the skills and time required, as well as the number of ingredients and tools needed. Adult help and supervision is required for all recipes.

Table of Contents

Notes to Kids and Parents.................4

MyPyramid.................5

Special Tips and Glossary 6

Conversion Chart 6

Kitchen Tools 7

EASY

Bread Bowl Chili.................8

Crazy Shapes Pizza.................10

Nutty Couscous.................11

Prepare-to-Share Salad.................12

Lazy Lasagna.................14

INTERMEDIATE

Cheesy Peas Pasta.................16

Salsa Cheese Bake.................18

Foil-Baked Fish.................20

Apple Cinnamon Pork Chops.................22

Tiny Turkey Loaves.................24

ADVANCED

Keep on Rollin' Meatballs.................26

Creamy Stuffed Potatoes.................28

Dip-and-Roll Chicken Strips 30

Index.................32

Nick Fauchald is the author of many children's books. After attending the French Culinary School in Manhattan, he helped launch the magazine *Every Day with Rachael Ray*. He is currently an editor at *Food & Wine* magazine and lives in New York City. Although Nick has worked with some of the world's best chefs, he still thinks kids are the most fun and creative cooks to work with.

Dear Kids,

Dinner is a great opportunity to spend time with your family and friends and share some great food! It's even more fun to cook it yourself. The recipes in this book are healthy and easy enough for you to make with only a little help from an adult.

Cooking is fun, and safety in the kitchen is very important. As you begin your cooking adventure, please remember these tips:

★ Make sure an adult is in the kitchen with you.
★ Tie back your hair and tuck in all loose clothing.
★ Read the recipe from start to finish before you begin.
★ Wash your hands before you start and whenever they get messy.
★ Wash all fresh fruits and vegetables.
★ Take your time cutting the ingredients.
★ Use oven mitts whenever you are working with hot foods or equipment.
★ Stay in the kitchen the entire time you are cooking.
★ Clean up when you are finished.

Now, choose a recipe that sounds tasty, check with an adult, and get cooking. Your friends and family are hungry!

Enjoy,
Nick

Note to Adults:

Learning to cook is an exciting, challenging adventure for young people. It helps kids build confidence, learn responsibility, become familiar with food and nutrition, practice math, science, and motor skills, and follow directions. Here are some ways you can help kids get the most out of their cooking experiences:

• Encourage them to read the entire recipe before they begin cooking. Make sure they have everything they need and understand all of the steps.

• Make sure young cooks have a kid-friendly workspace. If your kitchen counter is too high for them, offer them a stepstool or a table to work at.

• Expect new cooks to make a little mess, and encourage them to clean it up when they are finished.

• Help multiple cooks divide the tasks before they begin.

• Enjoy what the kids just cooked together.

MyPyramid

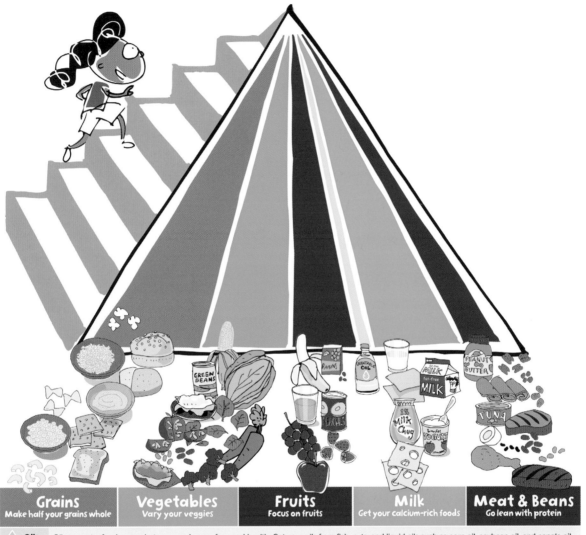

Grains	Vegetables	Fruits	Milk	Meat & Beans
Make half your grains whole	Vary your veggies	Focus on fruits	Get your calcium-rich foods	Go lean with protein

◊ **Oils** — Oils are not a food group, but you need some for good health. Get your oils from fish, nuts, and liquid oils such as corn oil, soybean oil, and canola oil.

In 2005, the U.S. government created MyPyramid, a plan for healthy eating and living. The new MyPyramid plan contains 12 separate diet plans based on your age, gender, and activity level. For more information about MyPyramid, visit *www.mypyramid.gov.*

The pyramid at the top of each recipe shows the main food groups included. Use the index to find recipes that include food from the food group of your choice, major ingredients used, recipe levels, and appliances/equipment needed.

Special Tips and Glossary

Cracking Eggs: Tap the egg on the counter until it cracks. Hold the egg over a small bowl. Gently pull the two halves of the shell apart until the contents fall into the bowl.

Measuring Dry Ingredients: Measure dry ingredients (such as flour and sugar) by spooning the ingredient into a measuring cup until it's full. Then level off the top of the cup with the back of a butter knife.

Measuring Wet Ingredients: Place a clear measuring cup on a flat surface, then pour the liquid into the cup until it reaches the correct measuring line. Be sure to check the liquid at eye level.

Bake: cook food in an oven

Chop: cut food into small pieces of similar size

Cool: set hot food on a wire rack until it's no longer hot

Cover: put container lid, plastic wrap, or aluminum foil over a food; use aluminum foil if you're baking the food, and plastic wrap if you're chilling, freezing, microwaving, or leaving it on the counter

Drain: pour off a liquid, leaving food behind; usually done with a strainer or colander

Fluff: stir rice or couscous with a fork

Grease: spread butter, cooking spray, or shortening on a piece of cookware so food doesn't stick

Line: cover the bottom of a baking sheet or pan with foil or parchment paper

Preheat: turn an oven on before you use it; it usually takes about 15 minutes to preheat an oven

Slice: cut something into thin pieces

Spread: to make an even layer of something soft, like mayonnaise or frosting

Sprinkle: to scatter something in small bits

Stir: mix ingredients with a spoon until blended

Whisk: stir a mixture rapidly until it's smooth

METRIC CONVERSION CHART

1/4 teaspoon (1 milliliter)
1/2 teaspoon (2.5 milliliters)
1 teaspoon (5 milliliters)
2 teaspoons (10 milliliters)

1 tablespoon (15 milliliters)
2 tablespoons (30 milliliters)
3 tablespoons (45 milliliters)
6 tablespoons (90 milliliters)

1/4 cup (60 milliliters)
1/3 cup (75 milliliters)

1/2 cup (125 milliliters)
3/4 cup (180 milliliters)
1 cup (250 milliliters)
1 1/2 cups (375 milliliters)
2 cups (500 milliliters)
3 cups (750 milliliters)

4 ounces (112 grams)
8 ounces (224 grams)
14 ounces (392 grams)
15 ounces (420 grams)
16 ounces (448 grams)

1/4 pound (113 grams)
1/2 pound (227 grams)
1 pound (454 grams)

TEMPERATURE CONVERSION CHART

350° Fahrenheit (175° Celsius)
375° Fahrenheit (190° Celsius)
400° Fahrenheit (200° Celsius)
425° Fahrenheit (220° Celsius)

Kitchen Tools

HERE ARE THE TOOLS YOU'LL USE WHEN COOKING THE RECIPES IN THIS BOOK ★

8-by-8-inch baking pan

9-by-13-inch baking pan

Aluminum foil

Baking sheet

Can opener

Colander

Cookie cutters

Cooking spray

Cutting board

Fork

Kitchen shears

Measuring cups

Measuring spoons

Melon baller

Microwave-safe bowls

Mini loaf pans

Mixing bowls

Oven mitts

Paring knife

Pizza cutter

Plastic wrap

Potato masher

Serrated knife

Small serving bowls

Small, sharp knife

Tongs

Whisk

Wire cooling rack

Wooden spoon

Spoon

7

Bread Bowl Chili

INGREDIENTS

16-ounce can black beans
16-ounce can kidney beans
4 sourdough buns
14-ounce can diced
   tomatoes with
   onions and garlic
4-ounce can diced
   green chilies
2 teaspoons lime juice
1 tablespoon chili powder
1 teaspoon cumin
1 teaspoon salt
1/4 teaspoon freshly
   ground pepper

TOOLS

Colander
Can opener
Serrated knife
Cutting board
Measuring spoons
Large microwave-safe bowl
Wooden spoon
Oven mitts

Place the colander in the sink. Pour the beans into the colander and rinse with water.

Ask an adult to cut off the top of each bun with the serrated knife.

Pull out chunks of bread from the inside of the bun, leaving a 1/2-inch-thick shell. Save the bread chunks to serve with the chili.

Pour the beans, tomatoes, chilies, lime juice, chili powder, cumin, salt, and pepper into a large microwave-safe bowl and stir.

8

NUTRITION NOTE★ Black beans and kidney beans are full of protein, which help the body build bones, muscles, and skin.

5

Ask an adult to heat the mixture, uncovered, in the microwave for 5 minutes. Stir well. Heat for 10 minutes more or until warmed through.

6 Spoon into the bread bowls and serve.

9

Crazy Shapes Pizza

INGREDIENTS
12-inch prepared
  pizza crust
5 slices cheese, such as
  cheddar or mozzarella
3/4 cup pizza sauce
15 slices pepperoni

TOOLS
Baking sheet
Cookie cutters or
  kitchen shears
Cutting Board
Measuring cups
Small spoon
Oven mitts
Pizza cutter

Preheat the oven to 400°. Place the pizza crust on a baking sheet.

Use your favorite cookie cutters to cut shapes out of the cheese slices or cut your own shapes with a kitchen shears.

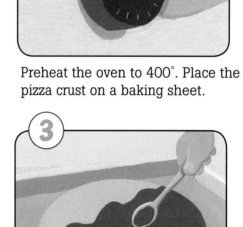

Spoon the pizza sauce over the crust, using the back of the spoon to spread it around.

Scatter the pepperoni on top of the pizza and top it with cheese.

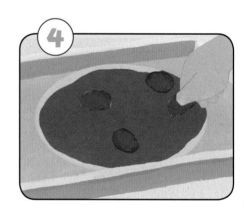

Ask an adult to bake the pizza for 12-15 minutes or until the crust is crispy and the cheese is melted. Let cool for 5 minutes.

6 Cut the pizza into wedges with the pizza cutter and serve.

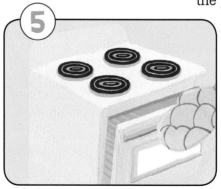

Nutty Couscous

Pour the couscous, chicken broth, and orange juice in a medium microwave-safe bowl and stir.

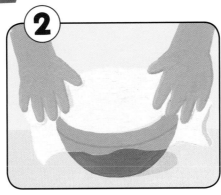

Cover the bowl with plastic wrap. Ask an adult to heat the couscous in the microwave for 4 minutes.

Fluff the couscous with a fork.

Add the cumin, salt, fruit, nuts, and oil to the couscous and stir.

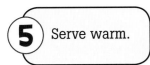

Serve warm.

INGREDIENTS

1 1/2 cups tri-color or
  plain couscous
1 1/2 cups chicken broth
3 tablespoons orange juice
1 teaspoon cumin
1 teaspoon salt
1 cup dried fruit, such as
  raisins, cranberries,
  and apricots
1 cup roasted almonds or
  other nuts
3 tablespoons extra-virgin
  olive oil

TOOLS

Medium microwave-safe bowl
Measuring cups
Measuring spoons
Wooden spoon
Plastic wrap
Fork

11

VEGETABLES

Prepare-to-Share Salad

INGREDIENTS

1 red or green bell pepper
1 cup mushrooms
1 cup diced ham
8-ounce bag mixed
    salad greens
1/2 cup sesame seeds
1 cup cherry tomatoes
1 cup canned chickpeas,
    drained
1/2 cup crumbled feta
    cheese
1 cup croutons
Assorted salad dressings
    (French, ranch, Italian)

TOOLS

Paring knife
Cutting board
Measuring cups
8 small bowls
Large mixing bowl

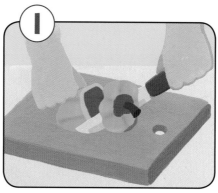

1 Wash the pepper and have an adult cut off the top. Scoop out the seeds and throw them away with the top.

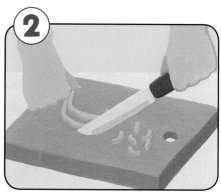

2 Have an adult chop the pepper into small chunks and place them in a small bowl.

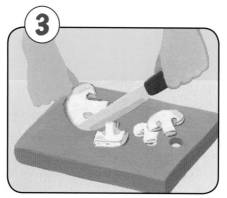

3 Wash the mushrooms and have an adult slice them. Place them in a small bowl.

4 Have an adult dice the ham. Place it in a small bowl.

12

HEALTHY CHOICE★ Add sliced chicken or steak to give this healthy salad a protein punch.

5

Pour the salad greens into a large mixing bowl.

6

Place the sesame seeds, tomatoes, chickpeas, cheese, and croutons in separate small bowls.

7 Serve buffet-style with the salad dressings.

GRAINS, MILK

Lazy Lasagna

INGREDIENTS
3 cups spaghetti sauce
8-10 dry lasagna noodles
15-ounce container
   ricotta cheese
8-ounce bag shredded
   mozzarella cheese

TOOLS
9-by-13-inch baking pan
Measuring cups
Large spoon
Oven mitts
Small, sharp knife

HEALTHY CHOICE★
Add fiber to your diet
by using whole-grain
noodles in all of your
pasta dishes.

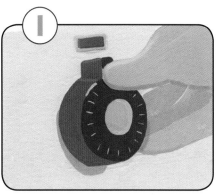

Preheat the oven to 375°.

Pour half of the spaghetti sauce over the bottom of the baking pan and spread with a spoon.

Place an even layer of lasagna noodles over the sauce. [NOTE: You may need to break the noodles to make them fit.]

Spoon half of the ricotta cheese over the noodles.

14

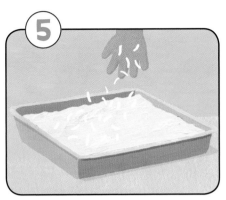

5

Sprinkle half of the mozzarella over the ricotta in an even layer.

6

Repeat steps 2-5 to build another layer of lasagna.

7

Ask an adult to bake the lasagna for 40 minutes. Let the lasagna cool for 15 minutes.

8 Cut into squares and serve.

This Recipe Includes

GRAINS, MILK, VEGETABLES

Cheesy Peas Pasta

INGREDIENTS

2 cups penne pasta

1 tablespoon extra-virgin olive oil

3 cups warm water

1 1/2 cups frozen peas and carrots

1 cup chicken broth

1/2 cup heavy cream

1/2 cup grated freshly Parmesan cheese

1/3 cup ricotta cheese

1/2 teaspoon salt

1/2 teaspoon freshly ground pepper

TOOLS

Measuring cups

Measuring spoons

2 medium mixing bowls

Wooden spoon

Colander

8-by-8-inch baking pan

Aluminum foil

Oven mitts

1

Put the pasta, olive oil, and warm water in a medium mixing bowl and stir.

2

Let the mixture stand for 30 minutes to soften the pasta.

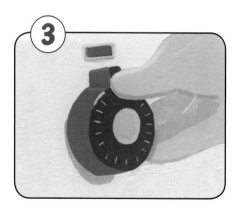

3

Preheat the oven to 400°.

4

In another medium mixing bowl, combine the vegetables, chicken broth, cream, Parmesan, ricotta, salt, and pepper and stir.

NUTRITION NOTE★ Plain frozen vegetables are just as healthy as fresh vegetables.

5

Set the colander in the sink. Pour the pasta into the colander and let the water drain.

6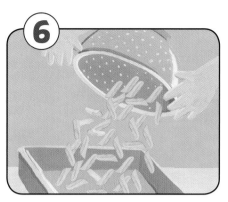

Pour the pasta into the baking pan.

7

Pour the vegetable mixture over the pasta and cover the pan with aluminum foil.

8

Ask an adult to bake the pasta for 35 minutes or until tender. Remove the foil and let pasta cool for 5 minutes.

9 Spoon into bowls and serve.

This Recipe Includes

MILK, GRAINS, MEAT & BEANS

Salsa Cheese Bake

INGREDiENTS
Two 6-inch corn tortillas
1 cup shredded Monterey
    Jack cheese
1 cup shredded cheddar
    cheese
5 eggs
1 cup milk
1 cup salsa
6 tablespoons sour cream,
    optional

TOOLS
Cooking spray
8-by-8-inch baking pan
Kitchen shears
Measuring cups
Large bowl
Whisk
Oven mitts
Paring knife
Measuring spoons

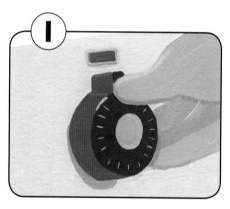

Preheat the oven to 350˚.

Grease the baking pan with the cooking spray.

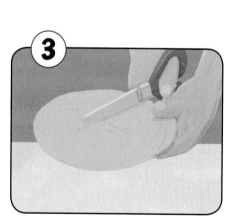

Cut the tortillas in half with the kitchen shears

Line the bottom of the baking pan with the tortillas. Sprinkle the cheeses over the tortillas in an even layer.

NUTRiTioN NOTE★ Eggs are very high in protein. Our bodies need protein to build muscle.

5 Place the eggs, milk, and salsa into a large bowl and whisk.

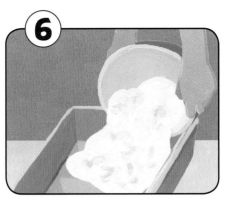

6 Pour the egg mixture over the cheese.

7 Ask an adult to bake the casserole for 40 minutes or until set. Let cool for 5 minutes.

8 Cut the casserole into squares and serve. Top each with a spoonful of sour cream, if desired.

This Recipe Includes
FRUITS, MEAT & BEANS

Foil-Baked Fish

INGREDIENTS

4 boneless, skinless
   tilapia fillets
1/4 cup jarred pesto
1 lemon
8 cherry tomatoes

TOOLS

Aluminum foil
Measuring spoons
Measuring cups
Serrated knife
Cutting board
Baking sheet
Oven mitts

Preheat the oven to 350°.

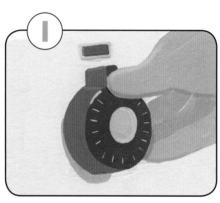

Tear off four pieces of aluminum foil, each about 12-by-16 inches. Place a fish fillet on the bottom half of each foil square.

Spread 1 tablespoon of pesto over the top of each piece of fish.

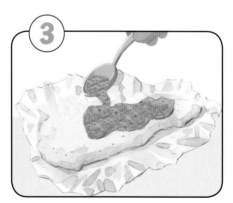

Ask an adult to cut the lemon into eight slices. Place two lemon slices on top of each piece of fish.

NUTRiTiON NOTE★ Fish is lower in calories, saturated fat, and cholesterol than many other sources of protein.

Ask an adult to cut the cherry tomatoes in half. Place four tomato halves on top of each piece of fish.

Fold the top half of the foil over each fish fillet. Fold up all four sides to seal each packet. Place the packet on a baking sheet. Repeat with the remaining foil and fish.

Ask an adult to bake the fish for 20 minutes. Let cool 5 minutes.

Open foil packets slightly, place on plate, and serve.

FRUITS,
MEAT & BEANS

This Recipe Includes

Apple Cinnamon Pork Chops

INGREDIENTS

4 apples
1/4 teaspoon ground
   cinnamon
1 tablespoon sugar
4 boneless pork chops
Pinch of salt
Pinch of freshly ground
   black pepper
2 tablespoons cold butter

TOOLS

Small, sharp knife
Cutting board
Melon baller
8-by-8-inch baking pan
Measuring spoons
Small mixing bowl
Aluminum foil
Oven mitts

1

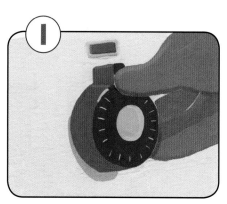

Preheat the oven to 350°.

2

Wash the apples and have
an adult cut them in half.
Use the melon baller to
remove the cores and stems.

3

Have an adult slice each apple
half into 1/2-inch wedges and
spread them on the bottom of
the baking pan.

4

Place the cinnamon and sugar
together in a small mixing bowl
and stir. Sprinkle the cinnamon
mixture over the apples.

22

NUTRITION NOTE★ Pork is a good source of a nutrient
called thiamin (also known as vitamin B1). This helps your
body turn protein, fat, and carbohydrates into energy.

Sprinkle both sides of the pork chops with salt and pepper, then place the pork chops on top of the apples.

Cut the butter into small cubes and scatter the cubes on top of the pork chops. Cover the baking pan with aluminum foil.

Ask an adult to bake the pork chops for 20 minutes. Remove the foil and bake for about 10 minutes more, until the pork is fully cooked. Let cool for 5 minutes.

8 Serve the pork chops and apples.

iNTERMEDiATE
Number of Servings: 4 (2 mini-loaves)
Ready to Eat: 1 hour and 10 minutes

This Recipe Includes
MEAT & BEANS

Tiny Turkey Loaves

INGREDiENTS

1 celery stalk
1 large egg
1/3 cup sour cream
1 cup bread crumbs
1/4 cup milk
2 tablespoons Dijon
   mustard
2 teaspoons salt
1 teaspoon freshly ground
   black pepper
1 pound ground turkey
1/4 cup ketchup
2 tablespoons brown sugar
1 tablespoon apple
   cider vinegar

TooLS

Paring knife
Cutting board
Large mixing bowl
Fork
Measuring cups
Measuring spoons
Wooden spoon
2 mini loaf pans
Small mixing bowl
Whisk
Spoon
Oven mitts
Serrated knife

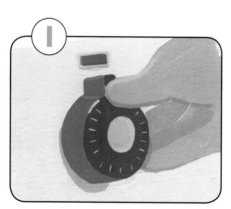

Preheat the oven to 375°.

Wash and dry the celery and have an adult chop it into small pieces.

Crack the egg into a large mixing bowl and beat it with a fork.

Add the celery, sour cream, bread crumbs, milk, mustard, salt, and pepper and stir.

24

Add the ground turkey and mix everything well with clean hands.

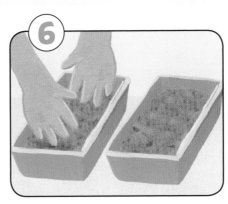

Press the mixture into two mini loaf pans.

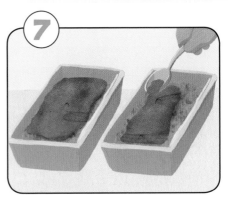

Pour the ketchup, brown sugar, and vinegar into a small mixing bowl and whisk. Spoon some of the ketchup mixture on top of each loaf.

Ask an adult to bake the loaves for 30 minutes. Spoon more ketchup mixture over the loaves and bake for 10 minutes more. Let cool for 10 minutes.

 Ask an adult to cut the loaves into slices and serve.

This Recipe Includes
MEAT & BEANS

Keep on Rollin' Meatballs

INGREDIENTS
1/2 pound ground beef
1/2 pound ground pork
1 large egg
1/3 cup breadcrumbs
1/4 cup freshly grated
   Parmesan cheese
1/2 teaspoon garlic powder
1/2 teaspoon salt
1 teaspoon Dijon mustard
1 cup pasta sauce, for serving

TOOLS
Aluminum foil
Baking sheet
Wire cooling rack
Measuring cups
Measuring spoons
Large mixing bowl
Oven mitts
Small serving bowl
Tongs

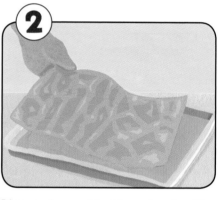

Preheat the oven to 375°.

Line a rimmed baking sheet with aluminum foil and place a wire rack on top of it.

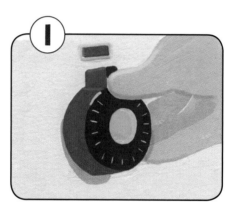

Place the beef, pork, egg, breadcrumbs, Parmesan cheese, garlic powder, salt, and mustard into a large mixing bowl and mix together with clean hands.

Wash your hands and leave them wet. Shape the meat mixture into 12 balls about the size of a golf ball. Place the meatballs on the rack.

26

5

Ask an adult to bake the meatballs for 30 minutes or until browned and fully cooked. Let cool for 5 minutes.

6 Pour the pasta sauce in a small serving bowl. Use tongs to place the meatballs on a serving plate. Serve the meatballs with pasta sauce.

This Recipe Includes

VEGETABLES, MILK, MEAT & BEANS

Creamy Stuffed Potatoes

INGREDIENTS
4 large baking potatoes
1/4 cup extra-virgin olive oil
1 1/4 cup shredded
     cheddar cheese
1 cup sour cream and
     onion dip
1/4 pound cubed, deli ham

TOOLS
Fork
Measuring cups
Small bowl
Serrated knife
Cutting board
Small spoon
Medium mixing bowl
Potato masher
Baking sheet
Oven mitts
Tongs

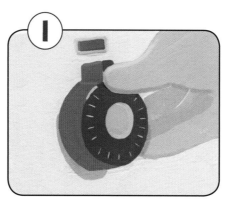

Preheat the oven to 375°.

Wash the potatoes; then pierce them all over with a fork.

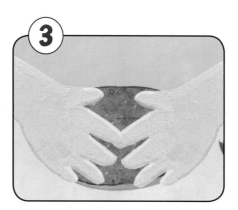

Pour the olive oil into a small bowl. Use your hands to rub the olive oil onto the potatoes. Ask an adult to cook the potatoes in the microwave for 12 minutes or until tender. Cool for 20 minutes.

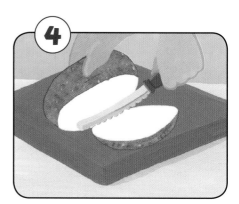

When the potatoes are cool enough to handle, ask an adult to cut about 1/4 inch off the top of each potato.

28

NUTRITION NOTE★ Don't forget to eat the skin! Potato skins are high in fiber, which helps you have a healthy digestive system.

5 Scoop out most of the inside (or flesh) of the potato with a spoon to form a shell. Place the potato flesh into a medium mixing bowl.

6 Add 1 cup of the cheese, the sour cream and onion dip, and the ham to the potato flesh and mash.

7 Fill the potato shells with this mixture.

8 Place the potatoes on the baking sheet and sprinkle with the remaining cheese.

9 Ask an adult to bake the potatoes for 15 minutes or until the cheese is melted and the potatoes are hot. Let cool for 10 minutes

10 Use tongs to place the potatoes on plates and serve.

GRAINS,
MEAT & BEANS

Dip-and-Roll Chicken Strips

INGREDIENTS

2 cups cornflakes cereal
1/4 cup grated Parmesan
  cheese
1/4 cup all-purpose flour
1 cup milk
1 pound chicken breast
  tenders
BBQ sauce or ketchup,
  for dipping

TOOLS

Baking sheet
Wire cooling rack
Aluminum foil
Measuring cups
Medium mixing bowl
Small mixing bowl
Oven mitts

Preheat the oven to 425°.

Line a rimmed baking sheet with aluminum foil and place a wire rack on top of the foil.

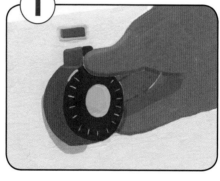

Place the cornflakes and Parmesan cheese in a medium mixing bowl. Smash and squeeze the cornflakes with your hands into coarse crumbs.

Pour the flour onto a plate. Pour the milk into a small mixing bowl.

5 Dip one chicken tender into the milk.

6 Roll it in the flour.

7 Dip it back into the milk.

8 Roll it in the cornflakes mixture to coat. Place the breaded chicken on the baking sheet. Repeat with all chicken tenders.

9 Ask an adult to bake the chicken tenders for 30 minutes or until crispy and cooked through. Let cool for 5 minutes.

10 Serve warm with BBQ sauce or ketchup.

INDEX

Advanced Recipes
    Creamy Stuffed Potatoes, 28–29
    Dip-and-Roll Chicken Strips, 30–31
    Keep on Rollin' Meatballs, 26–27
Apple Cinnamon Pork Chops, 22–23
apples, 22
beans, 8
bell peppers, 12
Bread Bowl Chili, 8–9
carrots, 16
celery, 24
cheese, 10, 12, 14, 16, 18, 26, 28, 30
Cheesy Peas Pasta, 16–17
chicken, 11, 12, 16, 30
chickpeas, 12
cooking time. See *Ready to Eat.*
cornflakes cereal, 30
couscous, 11
Crazy Shapes Pizza, 10
cream, 16
Creamy Stuffed Potatoes, 28–29
dairy, 10, 12, 14, 16, 18, 24, 28, 30
Dijon mustard, 24, 26
Dip-and-Roll Chicken Strips, 30–31
Easy Recipes
    Bread Bowl Chili, 8–9
    Crazy Shapes Pizza, 10
    Lazy Lasagna, 14–15
    Nutty Couscous, 11
    Prepare-to-Share Salad, 12–13
eggs, 18, 24, 26
fish, 20
food groups
    fruits, 11, 20, 22
    grains, 8, 10, 11, 14, 16, 18, 30
    meat & beans, 8, 10, 11, 18, 20, 22, 24, 26, 28, 30
    milk, 10, 14, 16, 18, 28
    vegetables, 12, 16, 28
food pyramid, 5
Foil-Baked Fish, 20–21
fruits, 8, 11, 20, 22
ground beef, 26
ground pork, 26
ham, 12, 28
Intermediate Recipes
    Apple Cinnamon Pork Chops, 22–23

Cheesy Peas Pasta, 16–17
    Foil-Baked Fish, 20–21
    Salsa Cheese Bake, 18–19
    Tiny Turkey Loaves, 24–25
juices, 8, 11
Keep on Rollin' Meatballs, 26–27
ketchup, 24, 30
Lazy Lasagna, 14–15
lemons, 20
limes, 8
meats, 10, 12, 22, 24, 26, 28, 30
milk, 18, 24, 30
mushrooms, 12
noodles, 14
nuts, 11
Nutty Couscous, 11
oils, 11, 16, 28
oranges, 11
ovens, 10, 14, 15, 16, 18, 19, 20, 21, 22, 23, 24, 25, 26, 27, 28, 29, 30, 31
pasta, 11, 14, 16
peas, 16
pepperoni, 10
pesto, 20
pizza crust, 10
pork chops, 22
potatoes, 28
preparation time. See *Ready to Eat.*
Prepare-to-Share Salad, 12–13
Ready to Eat
    15 minutes, 10, 12
    25 minutes, 11
    40 minutes, 8
    45 minutes, 20
    55 minutes, 22
    1 hour, 14, 18, 26, 28, 30
    1 hour 10 minutes, 24
    1 hour 30 minutes, 16
salad dressing, 12
salad greens, 12
salsa, 18
Salsa Cheese Bake, 18–19
sauces, 10, 14, 26, 30
serving sizes
    serves four, 8, 10, 11, 12, 20, 22, 24, 26, 28, 30
    serves six, 18

serves eight, 14
serves twelve, 16
sesame seeds, 12
sour cream, 18, 24
sourdough buns, 8
spaghetti sauce, 14, 26
tilapia, 20
Tiny Turkey Loaves, 24–25
tomatoes, 8, 12, 20
tools
    aluminum foil, 7, 16, 20, 22, 26, 30
    baking pans, 7, 14, 16, 18, 22
    baking sheets, 7, 10, 20, 26, 28, 30
    bowls, 7, 8, 11, 12, 16, 18, 22, 24, 26, 28, 30
    can openers, 7, 8
    colanders, 7, 8, 16
    cookie cutters, 7, 10
    cooking spray, 7, 18
    cutting boards, 7, 8, 10, 12, 20, 22, 24, 28
    forks, 7, 11, 24, 28
    kitchen shears, 7, 10, 18
    knives, 7, 8, 12, 14, 18, 20, 22, 24, 28
    measuring cups, 7, 10, 11, 12, 14, 16, 18, 20, 24, 26, 28, 30
    measuring spoons, 7, 8, 11, 16, 18, 20, 22, 24, 26
    melon ballers, 7, 22
    microwave-safe bowls, 7, 8, 11
    mini loaf pans, 7, 24
    mixing bowls, 7, 12, 16, 22, 24, 26, 28, 30
    oven mitts, 7, 8, 10, 14, 16, 18, 20, 22, 24, 26, 28, 30
    pizza cutters, 7, 10
    plastic wrap, 7, 11
    potato mashers, 7, 28
    spoons, 7, 8, 10, 11, 14, 16, 24, 28
    tongs, 7, 26, 28
    whisks, 7, 18, 24
    wire cooling racks, 7, 26, 30
    wooden spoons, 7, 8, 11, 16, 24
tortillas, 18
turkey, 24
vegetables, 8, 12, 16, 24, 28

ON THE WEB

FactHound offers a safe, fun way to find Web sites related to topics in this book. All of the sites on FactHound have been researched by our staff.

1. Visit *www.facthound.com*
2. Type in this special code: 1404839984
3. Click on the FETCH IT button.

Your trusty FactHound will fetch the best sites for you!

KIDS DISH

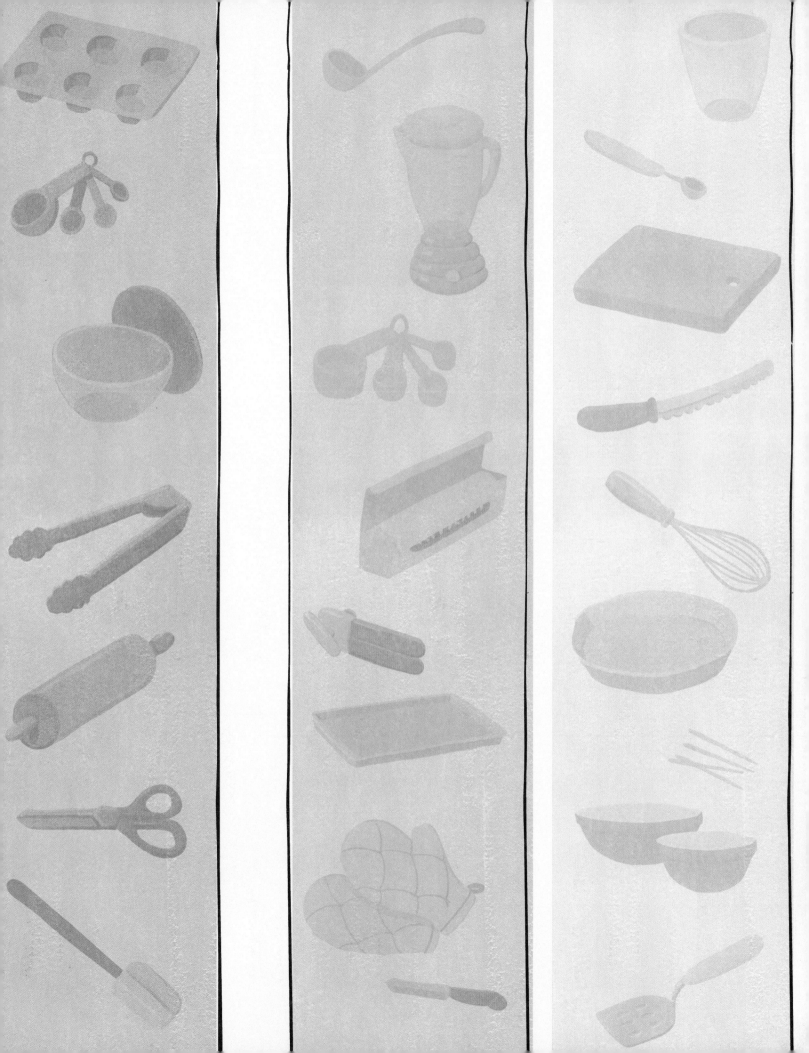

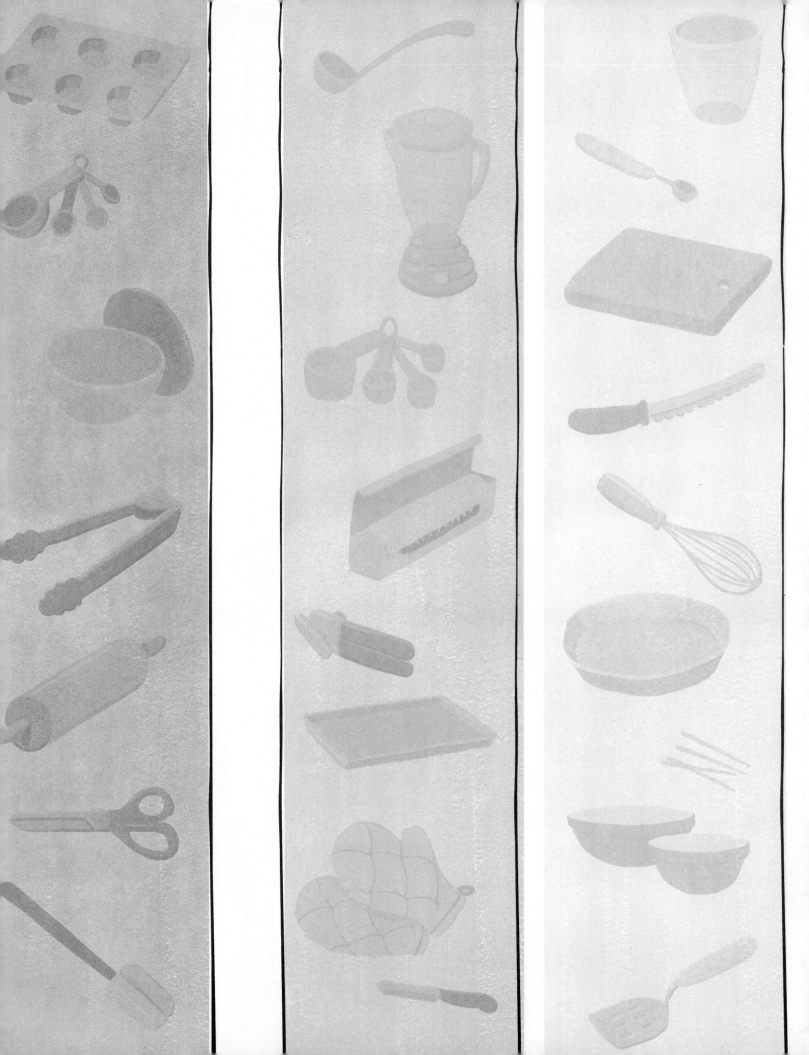